A Book of Hugs

Hug (həg), *v.*, hugged, hug•ging —*v.t.* 1. To clasp a person or thing in one's arms; to embrace [? Scand; cf. Icel *hugga* to soothe, console; akin to OE *hogian* to care for] —*n.* an embrace

Hugger, _n._, one who hugs —Ant., huggee [Obs.] a person or thing that receives a hug

Huggable, _adj._, possessing an affectionate nature or qualities desirable to hug —Ant., unhuggable

A Book of Hugs

by Dave Ross

illustrated by Laura Rader

SCHOLASTIC INC.
New York Toronto London Auckland Sydney
Mexico City New Delhi Hong Kong

For Mom & Dad
(who taught me how to hug) —D.R.

For my "sister" Lyn, expert at the
single-arm hug, with love —L.R.

ISBN 0-439-10989-2

Text copyright © 1980, 1999 by Dave Ross.
Illustrations copyright © 1999 by Laura Rader. All rights reserved.
Published by Scholastic Inc., 555 Broadway, New York, NY 10012,
by arrangement with HarperCollins Children's Books, a division of
HarperCollins Publishers. SCHOLASTIC and associated logos are
trademarks and/or registered trademarks of Scholastic Inc.

12 11 10 9 8 7 6 5 4 3 2 1   0 1 2 3 4 5/0

Printed in the U.S.A.   09

First Scholastic printing, January 2000

Typography by Al Cetta.

Newly Illustrated Edition

There are all kinds of hugs in the world. . . .

PUPPY HUGS

Puppy hugs are very soft and wet.

BEAR HUGS

Bear hugs are very strong. Be careful not to hurt.

OCTOPUS HUGS

An octopus hugs with its whole body.

FISH HUGS

Fish hugs are very cold and seldom returned.

P.S. Never hug a shark.

PORCUPINE HUGS

Porcupine hugs are done very carefully.

FRAIDYCAT HUGS

Fraidycat hugs make you feel safe.

PIGGYBACK HUGS
Sometimes called riding piggyback.

A good way to travel or see a parade.

MOMMY HUGS

You can never hug a Mommy too much.

DADDY HUGS

Daddy hugs are best when he first walks in the door.

BROTHER HUGS

Usually called a buddy hug.

Note: A circle of buddy huggers is called a huddle.

GRANDPA HUGS

Grandpa hugs are sometimes given while sitting.

GRANDMA HUGS

Grandma hugs can be found anywhere, but are especially nice in the kitchen.

SISTER HUGS

Also known as a single-arm hug.

Single-arm hugs are good for when you
walk together
(even if you aren't sisters).

BABY HUGS
Baby hugs are given with a little tickle.

GREAT-AUNT MARY HUGS

A Great-Aunt Mary hug can be given
only once a year.

(You will usually end up with lipstick on your cheek.)

ARM HUGS

Arm hugs are good if you are too little to get your arms around someone.

HAND HUGS
Usually called shaking hands.

Never hand-hug with dirty hands
unless you both have dirty hands.

KNEE HUGS

Knee hugs are good if you are tall.

Warning:
Never try
to knee-hug
someone who
is moving.

BLANKET HUGS

Everyone needs some kind of blanket.

TREE HUGS

Some trees are easier to hug than others.

Note: If you hug a pine tree
too long, you get stuck on it.

ROCK HUGS

Rock hugs are very hard on your face.

ICE-CUBE HUGS

Ice-cube hugs are quite common in February.

LAMPPOST HUGS

A lamppost hug can save you from
a painful experience.

SANDWICH HUGS

The whole family can get into a sandwich hug.

BIRTHDAY HUGS

A birthday hug is a present anyone can afford.

REPORT CARD HUGS

A Hug

Bee Hug

Sea Hug

HURT HUGS

Hurt hugs make the pain go away.

GOOD-NIGHT HUGS

Also sleep-tight and don't-let-the-bedbugs-bite hugs.

All hugs are wonderful, but
the best hugs of all are . . .

I-love-you hugs.

FACTS & HINTS ABOUT HUGGING

There is no such thing as a bad hug: there are only good hugs and great hugs.

Hug someone at least once a day and twice on a rainy day.

Hug with a smile; closed eyes are optional.

A snuggle is a longish hug.

Bedtime hugs help chase away bad dreams.

Never hug tomorrow when you could hug today.